Library of Congress Catalog Card No. 85-40536

Library of Congress Cataloging in Publication Data

Jennings, Linda M.
  The golden goose.

  Summary: Simpleton's generosity helps him gain a
princess for his bride.
  [1. Fairy tales. 2. Folklore—Germany] I. Grimm,
Jacob, 1785–1863. The golden goose. I. Ursell,
Martin, ill. III. Title.
PZ8.J372Go   1985   398.2′1′0943   [E]   85-40536
ISBN 0-382-09147-7

Text copyright © 1985 Hodder and Stoughton Ltd
Illustrations copyright © 1985 Martin Ursell
First published 1985

Text by Linda M. Jennings

**First published in Great Britain
1984 by Hodder & Stoughton Children's Books.**

Adapted and published, 1985, in the United States
by Silver Burdett Company,
Morristown, New Jersey.

Printed in Italy

THE BROTHERS GRIMM

THE GOLDEN GOOSE

Illustrated by
MARTIN URSELL

Text by Linda M. Jennings

SILVER BURDETT
MORRISTOWN, NEW JERSEY

There was once a man who had three sons. Now one day the eldest son went into the forest to cut wood, taking with him some rich cake and a bottle of fine wine. When he reached the best part of the forest, he sat down. No sooner had he brought out his food and drink – for he intended to have a good meal before he began his task – than a little gray man appeared, and begged to share it with him. "Indeed you won't," retorted the eldest son, "for if I give to you then there will be less for me – be off with you."

The youth finished his meal, and began his task of chopping down a tree. But as he swung the axe towards the trunk he missed, cutting his own arm instead, and was forced to return home.

"We still need the firewood," said the second son to his father. "Let me finish the job my brother was forced to abandon."

So the second son set out merrily, with a good meal of cake and wine in his bag. Like his brother before him he met the little gray man, and he, too, refused to share his meal. After he had eaten he found the tree that his brother had started to chop down, and with a will he set to work. Alas, the axe missed the tree and cut his leg, so that he, too, returned home, wounded.

Now the youngest son was known to the family as Simpleton, because he was thought to be a fool. Imagine, then, the derision when he now pleaded to be allowed into the forest to cut wood. "Well, if you want to kill yourself, go," said his father at last. So Simpleton went, but instead of the fine food his brother had received he was given some flat beer and cake mixed with ashes. But, unlike his brothers, when he met the little gray man Simpleton eagerly offered him some of his meager meal.

The two of them sat down and shared the food, which immediately turned to good rich cake and fine wine as they sampled it.

"You have shown me more kindness than both your brothers together," said the little gray man, "and for this I will reward you. At the foot of yonder tree dig deep and you will find something of value." At these words he disappeared.

"I can but try," said Simpleton to himself, and he followed the little man's instructions. To his amazement, from the roots of the tree emerged a goose with feathers of the purest gold.

Simpleton was loath to return home with his wonderful goose, so he walked on until he came to an inn where he decided to spend the night. Now the landlord had three daughters, whose eyes gleamed with curiosity and greed when they caught sight of the golden goose. While Simpleton lay asleep the eldest one snatched at a feather, meaning to pluck it out. Instead her hand stuck to the goose, and however hard she tried she could not pull it away. "Let me help you, sister," said the second girl, but she stuck fast to her sister's gown. The two sisters screamed a warning to the third one, but too late! As she took hold of her sister's arm she became as firmly stuck as the other two.

In the morning Simpleton set out from the inn with the goose tucked under his arm, not noticing the three girls, each stuck fast behind him. Very soon he met the Parson, who was shocked to see the three girls following a young man. "Are you not ashamed to chase a man in this bold fashion?" he cried, catching hold of the youngest sister. Well, you know what happened then! Parson, too, stuck fast!

As they continued on into the country they met the Sexton. "Why are you leaving town?" he cried to the Parson. "There's a christening this afternoon." He held out his hand to catch at the Parson's coat – and he, too, stuck fast and was forced to follow the strange little procession. They soon reached some open fields where two peasants were tilling the soil. "Help us, dear friends," called the Sexton. "If you just tug at my arm you will release me." But of course they couldn't, and now there were seven people all, despite themselves, running behind Simpleton.

At long last Simpleton and his line of followers reached the city. The King of that country had a very beautiful but solemn daughter who had never been known to smile. In desperation the King promised her hand in marriage to the first man who could make his daughter laugh. None succeeded.

It so happened that as the Princess was traveling through the city in her carriage she caught sight of Simpleton with the golden goose, and with a motley little crowd of people all running after him stuck fast to one another. And for the first time ever she laughed until the tears came to her eyes.

But the King had no wish to give his daughter to such a simple-looking fellow. "You can marry the Princess," he said, "provided you can bring me a man capable of drinking a whole cellar full of wine." At once Simpleton thought of the little gray man who had started him on his fortunes. He hurried back to the spot where the little gray man was last seen, only to find another man sitting on the tree-trunk instead. This fellow looked so woebegone that Simpleton asked what ailed him.

"Ah me," sighed the man, "I have such a terrible thirst that even the sweetest water cannot quench it, and a cask of wine can scarce wet my lips."

Simpleton could hardly believe his ears. "I can soon cure that," he cried, and took the man back to the Palace where the cellar full of wine had been prepared, and the man drank and drank to his heart's content.

Imagine the King's anger when at the end of the day every drop of wine had been drunk. "Of course you can marry my daughter," said the King, swallowing his rage, "but only on condition that you find someone capable of consuming a mountain of bread."

Straightaway Simpleton returned to the forest, and this time he found a fellow who was moaning and groaning with hunger. "Come with me," said Simpleton, "for I can lead you to enough bread to feed an army." Once again the King was thwarted, for by the end of the day the hungry man had eaten every last crumb of the huge bread mountain. But when Simpleton asked for the hand of the Princess for the third time, the King demanded that he should bring to the Palace a ship capable of sailing on land as well as on water.

When Simpleton returned to the forest he found the little gray man himself. "What shall I do?" asked Simpleton, "for if I am to win the hand of the Princess I am to take the King a ship that can sail on land and water alike."

"I have both ate and drunk for you," said the little gray man, "but because of your kindness to me I shall grant you this third request." So Simpleton returned to the Palace with a wonderful ship that could sail on both land and water.

The King could no longer withhold his promise. Simpleton and the Princess were duly married, and when the King died they inherited the Kingdom and lived happily ever after. But Simpleton never forgot that he owed his good fortune to the little gray man.

2